What's Your Story?

Icebreaker Questions for Small Groups

Cheryl Shireman

DEDICATION

This book is dedicated to Steve Gladen, the Pastor of Small Group Community at Saddleback Church. Thank you for believing in me and for giving me an opportunity to serve God with you. It has been a wild ride!

CONTENTS

We are lonesome animals. We spend all our life trying to be less lonesome. One of our ancient methods is to tell a story begging the listener to say - and to feel - "Yes, that's the way it is, or at least that's the way I feel it. You're not as alone as you thought." John Steinbeck

From Steinbeck: A Life in Letters
Edited by Elaine Steinbeck and Robert Wallsten
Penguin Books – New York

ACKNOWLEDGMENTS

Thank you to Bill Lyne and Mark Weston for giving me my first opportunity to lead a small group ministry.

Thank you to the women in my small group:
Pat Dahms
Dianne Geeting
Kathy Kraszewski
Jeanne Parks
Cindy Schlaifer
Lisa Sells
Karen Slaubaugh
Lisa Smith
Shelia Spiece
Gayle Straley
Nicole Summers
Mary Weidner

and Carla Boggs and Connie Zerkle

Thank you for showing me God's love.
You are, literally, gifts from God.
I love you.

HOW TO USE THIS BOOK

You do not know a person until you know their story. We each have a story and it is filled with both factual details and personal details. I believe the amount we are willing to reveal to another is in direct proportion to the amount they are able to love us. You cannot love what you do not know.

When a group of people get together, one of the quickest and easiest ways to get to know one another is through the use of questions that prompt us to tell our story. That is the purpose of this book. The material is divided into three sections.

Getting to Know You is a series of factual questions that will allow you to know someone at a surface level.

 Getting to Know What You Think questions are a bit deeper and allow you to begin to know a person's experiences as well as their thoughts on various subjects.

Getting to Know What You Feel are a series of questions that often require a bit more of thought and reflection before answering.

New groups might want to start near the front of the book with questions that are easier to answer.

You may ask the questions in a variety of ways:

- Ask everyone in the group the same question
- Have group members open to a random page and answer the first question they see
- Have group members open to a random page and ask another group member the first question they see

You may also use the book in a variety of circumstances:

- As an icebreaker for new groups
- A fun break for groups that have been together a long time
- As a "get to know you" session whenever a new person is added to the group
- The first few minutes of every group meeting

There are only two rules that come with these questions:

1. Always let people "pass" and not answer a question
2. Have fun!

I hope these questions help your group members to know one another on a deeper level. So that you might love one another on a deeper level.

Cheryl Shireman

By this everyone will know that you are my disciples, if you love one another.

John 13:35 NIV

SECTION 1
GETTING TO KNOW YOU

What is your middle name and do you like it?

What is your favorite color?

What is one of your favorite songs?

Can you whistle?

What is your favorite flavor of ice cream?

What was the last movie you watched?

When you enter a room, what word do you use to greet people?

What song do you hate?

Where did you go to high school?

Can you wiggle your ears?

What is your favorite flavor of chewing gum?

Who is your favorite actor?

What is your favorite breed of dog?

Can you arch one brow?

What was the last television show you watched?

What is your favorite sport?

What household chore do you most enjoy?

How many states have you been to?

Can you crack your knuckles?

Who is your favorite actress?

What side of the bed do you sleep on?

Do you stand or walk on escalators?

What is the worst movie you have ever seen?

What is your favorite soda?

What was the last book you read?

What is your favorite pie?

What is your favorite cereal?

What is your favorite color?

What was the last magazine you read?

What is your favorite beverage?

What is your favorite tv show of all time?

What was the first movie you ever saw in a movie theater?

What is your favorite meal?

How long have you been living in your present home?

Who is your favorite singer?

What household chore do you least enjoy?

What is your middle name?

Do you prefer sweet or salty foods?

Do you still have your tonsils?

What is your favorite lunchmeat?

Cheryl Shireman

As a kid, did you have a stereo in your bedroom?

What type of food could you eat every day of your life?

What is your favorite dessert?

Do you enjoy crossword puzzles?

Which do you enjoy more – sunrise or sunset?

What do you do for a living?

What is your favorite soup?

Have you ever bungee jumped?

What was the last thing you ate?

Who is the last person you talked to on the phone?

Do you like scary movies?

What color is your house?

How far do you commute to work?

Do you fish or hunt?

If you have siblings, where are you in birth order?

Do you sleep with one or two pillows?

What do you buy in bulk?

What do you love about your job?

What is the first song you ever bought?

Do you like to play cards?

What is your favorite Thanksgiving food?

Do you like to camp?

What color is your car?

What is your favorite cookie?

What do you hate about your job?

As a kid, did you have a tv in your bedroom?

At what temperature is your home thermostat set?

What do you like on your pizza?

Have you read all of the books written by any single author?

How many countries have you been to?

Do you like spicy food?

When was the last time you slept in a tent?

What color is your bedroom?

What type of music do you like?

Do you like to do jigsaw puzzles?

How much cash do you normally carry with you?

Do you recycle?

Who was your favorite teacher and why?

Which do you prefer - thin crust or thick crust pizza?

What is your favorite board game?

Do you like to have your picture taken?

How long have you been working in your present job?

What is your favorite sandwich?

Are you right-handed or left-handed?

What is your favorite snack?

What is your least favorite board game?

SECTION 2
GETTING TO KNOW WHAT YOU THINK

What one word would you use to describe your home?

What bones have you broken, and how?

Are you more of a rose or daisy?

When was the last time you were on an airplane?

Can you start a campfire?

Have you ever given anyone a surprise party?

If you had a boat, what would you name it?

Do you make quick decisions?

Do you speak any foreign languages?

What is your favorite line from a movie?

Did you rebel as a teen, and if so, how?

Do you like roller coasters?

Are you a good cook?

What is your favorite kind of animal?

Do you feel most creative in the morning or evening?

Who is one of your favorite writers?

Do you make your bed every day?

How many books do you own?

Do you have a nickname?

What is a waste of time?

How do you reward yourself?

What is one steadfast rule in your home?

Have you ever had stitches?

How many albums or cds do you own?

How many movies on dvd or other form do you own?

Can you play chess?

As a teenager, what posters did you have on your walls?

When was the last time you were on a boat?

Are you a good listener?

What is your favorite kind of cheese?

How do you express your creativity?

Cheryl Shireman

Has anyone ever given you a surprise party?

Do you like to learn new things?

What is your favorite comic strip?

Are you good at checkers?

What is your favorite thing to cook?

Are you a good friend?

What is your favorite state?

What is your favorite kind of pen or pencil to write with?

What is your favorite color of crayon?

18

What is your favorite sound?

When was the last time you were on a train?

Are you more of a sturdy oak or bending willow?

As a child were you in the Girl Scouts or Boy Scouts?

Are you a good parent?

Are you good at tic tac toe?

What food do you typically eat for breakfast?

When was the last time you were on a subway?

Can you paint a room?

When was the last time you colored in a coloring book?

Do you snore?

Are you good at keeping a secret?

What color do you wear most often?

What is your favorite small town?

What is your favorite color of ink to write with?

What was the last thing you broke?

Can you change a tire?

When was the last time you were on a bus?

What sound do you hate?

Are you a good mechanic?

Are you fine china or paper plate?

Do you mail birthday cards to friends and/or family?

Are you self-disciplined or lacking in self-discipline?

Do you like to garden? Vegetable or flower or both?

What is your favorite fast food?

What is your favorite scent?

Are you good at computer repair?

When was the last time you were on a motorcycle?

Can you bake a cake?

Are you more of a saver or a spender?

Is your office or work space messy or organized?

Can you split firewood?

Are you good at interior design?

What is the next book you are planning to read?

Do you send hand-written letters or emails?

What is your favorite waste of time?

What habit do you have that drives others crazy?

Can you toss a football?

What was your favorite subject in school?

Do you have any allergies?

Have you ever operated a chainsaw?

Do you like to sing in public?

What tv show do you think is funny?

What do you hate the scent of?

Can you swim?

Do you like to sing in private?

Are you simple or complex?

Have you ever operated a bulldozer?

When was the last time you were on a bicycle?

What was your favorite thing to play as a child?

Do you like to dance?

Have you ever driven a tractor?

Have you ever surfed?

Are you a short-story or full-length novel?

Do you play any type of computer or video game?

Who mows the lawn at your house?

What is your favorite large city?

Have you ever ridden a horse?

Can you dunk a basketball?

Are you more of a morning person or night person?

What was your least favorite subject in school?

Can you ice skate?

When is your birthday?

Who is your favorite comedian?

Can you roller skate?

Are you more organized or haphazard?

Can you snow ski?

If you could only watch one tv show for the rest of your life, what show would it be?

Are you more thoughtful or forgetful?

Can you water ski?

What is your dream car?

Are you more of a crockpot or blowtorch?

What is your least favorite fast food?

How many hours do you spend on the computer per day?

What is the worst thing you have ever tasted?

Can you snowboard?

What is your favorite country to visit?

What perfume or cologne do you wear?

How many snacks do you eat in one day?

Can you ride a bike?

Have you ever ridden an elephant?

27

Are you more of a steady flame or crackling fire?

Can you skateboard?

As a child, was your room neat or messy?

Are you more of a sports car or mini-van?

Can you rollerblade?

What food do you typically eat for lunch?

Are you more of a luxury car or a SUV?

Can you ride a unicycle?

If you could live in any style home, what would you choose?

Are you more of a bicycle or motorcycle?

As a teen, did you have a crush on any celebrity?

What is the worst thing you have ever smelled?

What tv show do you watch on a regular basis?

How long does it take you to get ready to go somewhere?

Where were you born?

Are you more of a cat person or a dog person?

What is your least favorite restaurant?

If you could look like any celebrity, who would you choose?

What one word would you use to describe your car?

Did you play any kind of sports in high school or college?

What is your favorite comfort food?

What is your favorite candy?

When you are alone in your car, what do you listen to?

Are you a blue sky full of sunshine or a dark sky full of stars?

What was one of your favorite pets?

How many hours do you typically work per week?

What concerts have you attended?

Are you more of a thinker or doer?

What is the first thing you do when you wake up?

Do you make New Year's resolutions?

What food do you typically eat for dinner?

If you could live in any location in the world, where would you choose?

What is one of your favorite books?

What plays have you attended?

Do you have any sort of athletic ability?

What games did you play as a child?

How many hours do you spend watching tv every day?

Where do you like to sit in a movie theater?

What is your favorite restaurant?

What is your favorite day of the week?

Have you ever driven a racecar?

How many emails do you send per day?

What is the last thing you do before going to sleep?

What one word would you use to describe your style of dress?

Who was your favorite playmate as a child?

What is your dream job?

Where would your dream vacation be located?

How many hours do you typically sleep every night?

If you rode the school bus, where did you sit – front, middle, or back?

Have you ever won an award?

What is your favorite hair color?

How many emails do you receive per day?

When was the last time you locked yourself out of your house or car?

What magazines do you subscribe to?

Do you ever wear a hat?

When you were a child, what did you want to be?

Where do you sit most often in your home?

What is your favorite website?

What is your favorite month of the year?

If you could afford to, what would you like to pay someone else to do for you?

As a toddler, did you have a favorite toy or blanket?

On average, how many hours do you spend reading every day?

What is your favorite eye color?

What is your favorite reality tv show?

Do you keep Christmas Cards or throw them away ?

What are your hobbies?

What time do you typically get up?

When was the last time you danced?

What one word would you use to describe your hair style?

How old would you like to live to be?

Are you easy to get along with or difficult to get along with?

Do you sleep on your side, stomach, or back?

What food do you hate?

Have you ever won any money?

Have you ever ridden a camel?

How long does it take you to fall asleep?

Have you ever won any type of competition?

Do you keep birthday cards or throw them away?

What is something that you always keep organized?

Do you read the newspaper?

What website do you use most often?

What was your first job?

Are you afraid to fly?

What time do you typically go to bed?

Do you collect anything?

Would you rather live in the city or country?

What is your favorite season?

What is your least favorite thing to do?

If you had to be one inch taller or shorter, which would you choose?

Do you like surprises?

What is your favorite section of the newspaper?

What was your best job ever?

If you could freeze your appearance at any age, what age would it be?

Are you usually early, on time, or late?

Do you have an eBook reader?

Is your purse or wallet messy or organized?

What would you like to change about your appearance?

What is your favorite thing to do?

Have you ever run for any type of public office?

Have you ever met anyone famous?

How do you react when someone is late?

What is your favorite movie soundtrack?

Did you ever skip school?

Did you ever run away from home?

What are you good at?

What family tradition would you like to see your children continue?

What chores did you have to do as a kid?

Do you sleep in on the weekends?

What tv show would you like to be on?

When was the last time you played hooky from work?

What is your most precious family heirloom?

When you were a kid, what was the first thing you did when you came home after school?

How did your parents meet?

What is the high point of your career?

What is the most physically demanding thing you've done?

What one thing would you like to change about your high school experience?

What was your worst job ever?

Did you go to prom, and if so, with who?

If you could go to any concert, what would you choose?

Who is your favorite cartoon character?

What movie had the most impact on your life?

What values did your parents instill in you?

What was your favorite childhood pet?

What object do you remember from your childhood?

What do you like least about your home?

Who is the most loving person you know?

What did your parents do for a living?

What was your favorite tv show as a teenager?

What object from your childhood home would you like to have right now?

What is the best concert you have ever attended?

If you had to choose between having eight children or no children, which would you choose?

If money were not a consideration what gift would you buy for a friend or family member?

Are you good at remembering birthdays?

Have you ever hitchhiked?

If you doodle with a pen or pencil, what do you doodle?

Do you make a wish before you blow out your birthday candles?

Have you ever written a fan letter?

What is the most unusual job you have ever had?

Where do you shop most often?

Are you more high-maintenance or low-maintenance?

Is it easy or difficult for you to make friends?

What is the low point of your career?

If you could possess the singing ability of any singer, who would it be?

Have you ever sang karaoke?

Where do you most like to read?

Have you ever quit a job?

If you had two spare hours, would you rather watch tv or spend them on your computer?

What celebrity's death saddened you the most?

How did you spend your summers as a kid?

Do you like or dislike change?

What is the most stressful job you have ever had?

If you won twenty million dollars in the lottery, what would be the first thing you would do?

Cheryl Shireman

Have you ever been in, or attended, a beauty contest?

What celebrity do you most resemble?

Have you ever picked up a hitchhiker?

Do you send text messages, and if so, about how often?

What super power would you like to have?

Would you rather swim in an ocean or in a pool?

What is one thing you always make time for?

Are you good in an emergency situation?

Have you ever wished on a star?

46

When flying, where do you like to sit?

What is the strangest thing you save?

Where do you see yourself in ten years?

Are you more high-energy or low-energy?

Do you seek or avoid eye contact?

What do you like most about your home?

Have you ever worked as a waiter or waitress?

Who is someone you would really like to be friends with?

Would you rather have a quiet life or an exciting life?

Have you ever been fired from a job?

What movie are you embarrassed to admit that you like?

Are you more mild-tempered or hot-tempered?

SECTION 3
GETTING TO KNOW WHAT YOU FEEL

What one word would you use to describe your personality?

How are you raising (or will you raise) your children differently from the way you were raised?

When was the last time you felt out of control?

When do you feel most alive?

What trait is most important in a friend?

What was one of the best phone calls you ever received?

Who brings out the best in you?

What topic is too serious to joke about?

If you could witness any event from the past, what would it be?

If you could learn to do anything what would you do?

If you had to change your first name, what would you change it to?

When was the last time you were nervous?

50

What did you learn this week?

When did you become an adult?

What is your hidden talent?

If you could go on a road trip with anyone, where would you go and who would you go with?

What is your favorite holiday?

What cartoon did you watch as a child?

What is on your bedside table?

What is your worst habit?

Who/what were you named after?

51

Are you physically strong?

What is your favorite thing to do on a rainy day?

What is your favorite part of your job?

Do you push the elevator button more than once?

If you won five million dollars would you quit your job?

If you could be any animal for a day, which would you choose?

If you could travel to any location for free, where would you go?

If you could choose one food to be zero calories, what would you choose?

Are you emotionally strong?

Who do you miss the most?

Have you ever given money to a homeless person?

What was the last movie that made you cry?

What is the most important quality in a mate?

What was your favorite thing about your childhood bedroom?

When was the last time you felt lonely?

If you could relive one year of your life, what year would you choose?

What is the nicest thing anyone has ever said about you?

Were you spanked as a child?

What lesson did you learn as a child?

Do you believe in love at first sight?

What one thing always makes your heart beat fast?

If your life was a book, what would be the title?

When you review your life, what amazes you the most?

What is the most adventurous thing you have ever done?

What self-defeating thought keeps you from living your best life?

What lesson does God have to teach you over and over again?

If you had five thousand dollars to spend on yourself in one store, what would you buy and in what store?

What is your favorite joke?

Do you have a tattoo?

What is the best thing about being in love?

What one thing would you change about your childhood?

Describe your favorite photo of yourself as a baby.

What is the best advice your mother ever gave you?

Is it ever okay to lie?

What is your most expensive luxury item?

What is the fastest you have ever driven a car?

What is one of the worst phone calls you have ever received?

What fear are you trying to overcome?

Who brings out the worst in you?

Have you ever had a recurring dream or nightmare?

What was the most life-changing event of your life?

If you had to lose one of your senses, which would you choose?

If you could live your life over, what would you do differently?

What is your life motto?

How easily do you forgive?

Are you an introvert or an extrovert?

What was the most difficult year of your life?

If money and time were not a consideration, where would you travel in the next year?

How many times per day do you look in a mirror?

What are three things you are most grateful for?

What is the worst thing about being in love?

Describe a time you laughed so hard you could not stop.

Have you ever served on jury duty?

When was the last time you received flowers?

What do you like to shop for?

What epitaph would you like on your tombstone?

What is your favorite quote?

How are you similar to your mother?

What do you always put off doing?

How do you relax?

If you were going to a costume party dressed as a fictional character from a book, who would it be?

What is the best gift you ever received?

Your house is on fire and you can only carry out one possession, what will it be?

Describe your favorite photo of yourself as a toddler.

What is the worst advice your mother ever gave you?

What social clique where you a part of during high school?

How do you celebrate Christmas?

What do you wish you had more of?

Are you more of a leader or follower?

Do you dye your hair?

Are you emotionally stable or moody?

If you could live inside of any movie, what movie would it be and what character would you play?

Have you ever driven a motorcycle?

Where did you go on your last vacation?

How many times a day do you comb or brush your hair?

What is your favorite song?

When was the last time you sent flowers?

Do you own any autographs?

What is the last fun thing you did with a child?

What do you wish you had less of?

If you have a problem, who can you call at 3 a.m.?

Besides your own home, where do you hang out?

Describe your favorite photo of yourself as a child.

Do you play any musical instrument?

What is the best gift you have ever given?

How are you different from your mother?

Do you wear eye glasses or contacts?

What is your most treasured piece of jewelry?

What is your favorite way to spend Sunday afternoon?

What is the best advice you father ever gave you?

What type of home improvement skills do you possess?

In what room of your house are you most comfortable?

What is your favorite item of clothing?

How do you celebrate Easter?

What is your most cherished possession?

What is your happiest memory of your mother?

What is the most difficult thing you have ever done?

How many speeding tickets have you received?

What was a time you got into trouble as a child or teen?

Who inspires you?

How are you similar to your father?

Which do you prefer – a long bubble bath or a quick shower?

Have you ever visited someone in a jail or prison?

What song would you like to have played at your funeral?

What is your proudest moment?

What game do you almost always win?

How do you want to be remembered?

Describe your favorite photo of yourself as a teen.

What is your saddest memory of your mother?

If you were stranded on deserted island, what luxury item would you want to have with you?

Are you living your best life, and if not, why not?

What book have you read multiple times?

Do you wear reading glasses?

Who has made the biggest impact in your life?

How do you celebrate Thanksgiving?

How do you celebrate Valentine's Day?

If a movie was made about your life, who would play the lead role?

What has been your greatest accomplishment?

What game do you almost always lose?

Where was your best vacation ever?

Do you observe a Sabbath every week?

How do you celebrate Halloween?

Are you more goal-oriented or people-oriented?

Who do you most admire?

What is the worst advice your father ever gave you?

What is your happiest memory of your father?

What do you have to continually remind yourself to do?

Would you rather be rich or famous?

Have you ever visited someone in a nursing home?

If you had to live on a deserted island for one month with five people, who would you choose?

If you could live inside of a tv show, which would you choose and what character would you play?

If you could play any musical instrument, which would you choose?

What one word would you use to describe your closest relationship?

What one thing do you want to accomplish before you die?

Describe your favorite photo of yourself as an adult.

How are you different from your father?

What do you spend most of your time thinking about?

How do you celebrate New Year's Eve?

What is the saddest memory of your father?

If you inherited ten million dollars, how would you spend it?

What is your best idea for a new invention?

What do you most regret?

What do you buy on impulse?

What is your pet peeve?

Do you tend to avoid conflict of face it head on?

When was the last time you visited someone in a hospital?

Where does most of your money go?

What one word would you use to describe what kind of friend you are?

Describe a time when you could not stop crying.

What is the easiest thing about being a Christian?

If you could switch lives with any celebrity, who would it be?

Do you have any phobias?

If you could choose any one of these talents, which would you choose: singing, writing, acting, artistic skill?

Where does most of your time go?

If you were stranded on deserted island, what book would you want to have with you?

If you could have lunch with any living person who would it be?

What drives you crazy?

If you could look ten years into the future, would you?

What has been your greatest failure?

Whose personality are you most like in this group?

What tv show do you never get tired of watching – even in reruns?

Describe a favorite photo of yourself with another person.

What is the toughest thing about being a Christian?

Are you the most like your father or your mother?

What biblical character do you most relate to?

When were you last afraid?

Whose personality are you the most different from in this group?

If you were going to a costume party dressed as a fictional character from a tv show, who would it be?

What is your greatest strength?

What one word would you use to describe your relationship with your mother?

What one word would you use to describe your relationship with your siblings?

If you could ask Jesus one question right now, what would it be?

If you were stranded on deserted island, what personal hygiene product would you want to have with you?

Finish this sentence – The one thing no one would guess about me is...

Which one of the Ten Commandments is toughest for you to follow?

If you could know the date of your death, would you want to?

What is your best memory of gym class?

If you were going to a costume party dressed as a fictional character from a movie, who would it be?

What one word would you use to describe your relationship with your father?

If you could bring any deceased person back to life for one day, who would it be?

What habit do you find most annoying?

Do you like being the center of attention?

What is your greatest weakness?

How would you like to spend your days when you retire?

What compliment would you most like to receive?

What one word would you use to describe your relationship with your grandparents?

What movie have you seen multiple times?

What emotion do you experience most often?

What do you always get away with?

If you could choose them, what would your last words be?

Have you ever volunteered anywhere?

When was the last time you were bored?

What do you avoid thinking about?

How often do you pray?

What one word would you use to describe your relationship with your best friend?

Once you get to heaven, what will be the first question you will ask God?

What are your spiritual gifts?

Do you have a favorite poem?

What is the best idea you ever had?

What one thing would you like to change about yourself?

How do you measure success?

What is your worst memory of gym class?

What is your favorite Bible verse?

Where do you pray most often?

If you were going to a costume party dressed as a real-life character (living or deceased), who would it be?

Use one word to describe every person in this group.

What one thing about yourself do you hope never changes?

Do you think it is necessary for a Christian to go to church, and why or why not?

If you could job shadow anyone in the world, who would it be?

Do you think it is necessary for a Christian to be a part of a small group?

Do you think it is necessary for a Christian to serve inside the church?

Besides the Bible, what book has helped you most in your spiritual growth?

Do you think it is necessary for a Christian to serve outside the church?

What is your earliest childhood memory?

What are you most afraid of?

What dream has come true for you?

What does the word *fellowship* mean to you?

How do you serve God?

What does the word *discipleship* mean to you?

What is one thing that you used to believe that you don't believe now?

How long have you been a Christian?

What lesson did you learn from your parents?

How do you love God?

How often do you read the Bible?

How do you serve others?

What do you think makes God very sad?

What does the word *ministry* mean to you?

Have you ever fasted?

What is the hardest part of the Bible for you to understand?

What do you think makes God very happy?

Have you ever gone on a mission trip?

What radio channel do you listen to?

What gifts do you believe God gave you to share with others?

How would you describe God in one word?

Who prays for you?

How do you love others?

What moment in your life would you like to replay?

What does the word *evangelism* mean to you?

How would you describe Jesus in one word?

What part of the Bible gives you the most comfort?

What tv shows do you always record?

If you were going on a mission trip next week, where would you go?

What does the word *worship* mean to you?

What do you do to feed your soul?

How do you share your God-given gifts with others?

How would you describe the Holy Spirit in one word?

What is the worst idea you ever had?

How often do you fast?

What one thing do you know is true?

Who do you pray for?

What moment in your life would you never want to relive?

What dream still has not come true for you?

If you knew the world was ending one year from now, what would you do differently?

What song best describes your life?

If the whole world was listening, what would you say?

If you could make everyone in the world do one thing, what would it be?

If you could offer a newborn baby one piece of advice, what would it be?

What are you holding on to that you need to let go of?

Questions for your entire group:

What could your small group do to make a difference in your church?

What could your small group do to make a difference in your community?

What could your small group do to make a difference in the world?

What can you do, right now, to make the world a better place?

What are you waiting for?

ABOUT THE AUTHOR

Cheryl Shireman grew up in the Midwest and came to Christ relatively late in life. She did her best to outrun God, but ultimately realized that no one is quite that fast. She gave her life to Christ in 2003. In 2004 she became the Director of Small Groups in the Indiana church where she came to Christ. In 2008, she became the Small Group Network Coordinator. Founded by Saddleback's Steve Gladen, the SGN is a network for leaders of small group ministry. Through her work with the SGN, Cheryl works to connect small group ministry leaders across the world so that they might build relationships, encourage one another, and share resources and ideas. She is passionate about discipleship and believes that intentional and focused small groups are powerful tools in that life-long process.

She holds a Master's degree in Christian Education and an undergraduate in Creative Writing. She is also the author of one novel, and two reference books on writing. She is married, has three children, and one adorable granddaughter. She enjoys backpacking in the Colorado Rockies and gathering with family at her Indiana lake home on the weekends.

Cheryl's website is www.cherylshireman.com

To join Small Group Network, go to www.smallgroupnetwork.com

CPSIA information can be obtained at www.ICGtesting.com
Printed in the USA
LVOW102125250113

317296LV00024B/895/P

9 781460 978757